Social Media for Nonprofits
Amplify Your Impact

Table of Contents

We do not have a choice on whether we DO social media, the question is how well we DO it.

— Erik Qualman

Chapter 1. Introduction

In an ever-evolving digital landscape, harnessing the power of social media can prove to be invaluable for nonprofit organizations. With our special report on "Social Media for Nonprofits: Amplify Your Impact," we provide the definitive guide to successfully navigate this sphere. Empower your cause with the influence of Facebook, Twitter, Instagram, and more. Learn how to captivate your audience, amplify your message, and ultimately, increase your ability to create change. Whether you're a seasoned social media guru or a novice looking to dip your toes into the online world, this cheerful and engaging report is packed with information and insights, designed to motivate and equip you with the knowledge to take your nonprofit to the next level. Dive in, and you'll find no better companion on your journey to amplify your impact through the magic of social media. Don't miss this opportunity to unlock the endless possibilities of the digital world!

Chapter 2. Understanding Social Media: A Brief Overview

Social media! It's indisputably a term that offers a wide range of reactions and perceptions. For some people, it's a networking powerhouse that's responsible for boosting friendships, catalyzing professional opportunities, and enabling a global dialogue. For others, it's a risky doorway to inappropriate content, virtual noise, or unchecked distraction. Regardless of where you fall on that spectrum of opinion, there's no denying that social media has indeed become vital to our contemporary life. As you begin your own journey into the world of social media, or if you're just trying to find ways to better leverage it for your nonprofit, you must first delve into understanding the basics of this digital beast.

2.1. The Basics: Defining Social Media

Social media refers to online communication platforms that enable people to connect and share information and content with others. Precisely, it provides a virtual environment where users can develop personal profiles, establish friendships and professional relationships, engage in discussions, share various forms of multimedia, and more. Facebook, Twitter, Instagram, LinkedIn, and others have grown from being unique tech start-ups to global powerhouses influencing everything from entertainment to politics.

2.2. Evolution and Impact of Social Media

Since its inception, social media has consistently evolved to meet the needs of users and to respond to societal changes. This online revolutionization started with simple platforms like Friendster and MySpace but quickly developed into the behemoths we see today. With each iteration, new functionality has been added - live video, stories, and even virtual reality are now common functions within these platforms, thus enabling an amplified way of communication and interaction. Their impact has been substantial and varied, from aiding in brand creation to stirring international political events.

2.3. Key Components of Social Media

Social media is made up of several key components that enable it to serve users in multiple ways.

1. Personal Profiles: These are individual users' pages where they can share personal information, post updates, and connect with others.

2. Networks: The interconnections between different users based on their relationships.

3. Community Pages: Public spaces related to specific interests or causes where people with similar interests can discuss and share content.

4. Business Profiles: These are used by businesses and organizations to communicate with followers, market themselves, share news, and respond to customer issues.

5. Paid Advertising: Most social media platforms have a monetization element that allows businesses to promote their products or services to targeted users.

2.4. The Most Common Social Media Platforms

Now, let's go into an overview of the most popular platforms that you'll likely encounter and possibly utilize for your nonprofit organization:

2.5. Facebook

As of 2021, Facebook is the largest social media network in the world, with over 2.5 billion active users worldwide. Created in 2004 by Mark Zuckerberg, Facebook was originally intended to be an online directory for college students. Today, it has grown into a platform where individuals, businesses, and organizations can connect with one another, share information and engage in dialogue.

2.6. Twitter

Founded in 2006, Twitter is a platform best known for its brevity. Users communicate in short messages called Tweets, which are limited to 280 characters. Twitter is often used for news consumption, amplifying causes, and facilitating dialogues. It's especially beneficial for organizations wanting to provide updates and spark conversation around specific topics.

2.7. Instagram

Owned by Facebook, Instagram is a photo and video sharing platform that has gained tremendous popularity, particularly among younger generations. For nonprofits, it can be a powerful tool to visually share your narrative and engage with supporters.

2.8. LinkedIn

LinkedIn, launched in 2003, is a professional networking platform where users can showcase their professional achievements, connect with colleagues, and explore job opportunities. For nonprofits, LinkedIn can be a powerful tool for recruiting volunteers and connecting with potential supporters.

Understanding social media is like understanding a living, breathing entity. It is continually evolving, changing, and growing based on the desires and needs of its users. As representatives of nonprofit organizations, it's crucial to remember that our journey into social media isn't about being everywhere and doing it all. Rather, it's about strategically selecting platforms that will help us connect with our audiences, share our message, and amplify our cause in the most effective ways. With this overview, you are on your way to not just understanding social media but capitalizing upon its power to create positive change.

Chapter 3. Building Your Nonprofit's Digital Identity

Creating a robust digital identity is imperative for nonprofit organizations in today's interconnected world. Through strategic planning, careful curation, and a deep understanding of your cause, you can foster a strong online persona that communicates your mission, values, and objectives effectively.

3.1. Establishing Your Brand Persona

Your digital identity begins with your brand persona. This persona is a summation of your nonprofit's mission, values, objectives, and culture. It's essentially how you want your organization to be perceived by the outside world, and it should resonate with your intended audience.

When mapping out your organization's persona, consider what you stand for and how that aligns with the interests and needs of your target demographic. Identify the core strengths, qualities, and values that set your nonprofit apart and express these qualities consistently across all online channels.

Furthermore, your brand persona must be authentic, relatable, and engaging. It should communicate a story, evoking emotion and inciting action. Engaging narratives can transform abstract missions into tangible visions, making it easier for your audience to connect with and support your cause.

3.2. Creating Consistent Branding Materials

Effective branding is not only about sharing your persona, but it's also about visual consistency. This includes your logo, typography, color scheme, imagery, and other visual elements that make your nonprofit recognizable.

Your branding materials must be uniform across all online platforms to ensure a cohesive and consistent user experience. A mismatched or inconsistent brand identity can confuse your followers and weaken your brand's credibility. A professional, polished, and consistent aesthetic, on the other hand, can enhance recognition and cultivate trust among your audience.

It's also crucial to create and abide by a style guide, which should outline your brand colors, fonts, logos, imagery style, as well as tone, voice and language guidelines. Every content piece, from tweets to blog posts, should adhere to this guide to maintain brand consistency.

3.3. Building Your Website

Your website is the cornerstone of your digital identity. It's a digital hub where visitors can learn about your mission, see the impact of your work, get involved, and make donations. Thus, it's important that your site is informative, easy to navigate and visually striking.

Key considerations when building your website include creating a user-friendly navigation, maintaining an intuitive and responsive design, and ensuring your site is optimized for mobile viewing. Your content should be well-organized and easy to digest, with clear calls to action to guide visitors towards desired activities, like donating, volunteering, or signing up for a newsletter.

Also, keep in mind the SEO (Search Engine Optimization) aspects. Use relevant key phrases and words that your potential donors or volunteers might use to search for causes like yours. This will help your website show up in search engine results, thereby increasing traffic and visibility.

3.4. Finessing Your Social Media Presence

Social media platforms provide a unique opportunity to engage with your audience on a more personal level. Choose your platforms thoughtfully based on where your target audience spends their time online.

Each platform has its own culture and preferred content format. For instance, Instagram is ideal for sharing impactful visual content while Twitter is a powerful platform for real-time communication and engagement. Tailor your content and messaging to suit the norms of each individual platform and you have an increased chance of resonating with your followers.

Remember to maintain an active presence, regularly sharing valuable content aligned with your mission, responding to comments and messages, and keeping followers updated on your cause.

By upholding a consistent, engaging and meaningful digital identity, your nonprofit organization can effectively communicate its mission, amplify its impact, engage with its audience, and attain its objectives in the digital arena. It's a sophisticated process, but by dedicating time, resources, and a deep understanding of your organization's identity and objectives, you'll build a digital identity that truly resonates.

Chapter 4. Strategic Planning: Setting Effective Goals on Social Media

Is it not said, 'if you don't know where you're going, any road will take you there'? Therefore, the first step of any successful social media campaign is strategic planning which entails setting clear, measurable, achievable, relevant, and time-bound (SMART) goals. These objectives act as a guide throughout your digital journey, serving as road markers that chart your progress and keep you on track. Even the possibility of having this considerable influence does not come easy, it requires a well-crafted and meticulously implemented strategy.

4.1. Laying the Foundation: Identifying Your Nonprofit's Objectives

From spreading awareness, encouraging donations, rallying volunteers, or building community, nonprofits use social media for a variety of reasons. However, it's imperative to identify what your organization aims to achieve. By identifying your broad objectives, you can tailor your social media strategy to reinforce these goals. The implementation of SMART goals provides a measurable means for progress tracking.

For example, your organization may have the general objective to 'raise awareness about climate change'. A SMART goal might be to 'increase followers on our Instagram page by 25% over the next six months to disseminate valuable information and drive engagement around climate issues.' This goal is specific, measurable, achievable, relevant, and time-bound. Thus, every aspect of your strategy from content creation to engagement efforts should be formulated with an eye poised towards achieving your SMART goals.

4.2. Understanding Your Baseline

Before embarking on this digital adventure, understanding where you currently stand is vital. Performing a social media audit would involve cataloguing your nonprofit's existing social media profiles, considering their efficacy, and identifying gaps that could be filled in your future strategy.

While reviewing each platform, be sure to note down your current number of followers, the engagement rate of posts, content style, and tone, among others. This baseline data aids in benchmarking your progress and setting realistic goals based on your nonprofit's history and capacity.

4.3. Developing a Tactical Plan

Armed with your SMART goals and baseline understanding, you can now begin to develop your tactical plan.

Your plan should consider the following elements:

- **Channels:** Decide on which platforms align best with your audience and overall objectives.
- **Content:** Identify the types of posts that would resonate with your audience and align with your mission.
- **Frequency:** Set a frequency pattern. Posting too often can lead to exhaustion, while too infrequently can bring disconnection.
- **Engagement Plan:** Determine ways to invite and foster interaction amongst your audience.

Your detailed plan becomes the chief blueprint of how your social media strategy manifests. Each aspect intricately leans into supporting your overall objectives in becoming a digital influence.

4.4. Setting up a Content Calendar

A content calendar brings structure to your tactical plan by organising your posting schedule, themes, and objectives. Delve into scheduled holidays, awareness days, and key dates related to your cause, using them as content pillars around which to plan your posts. This method gives assurance your content remains relevant and timely.

Further, the regularity in posting boosts your nonprofit's visibility and strengthens relationships with your audience.

4.5. Monitoring and Adjusting

A social media strategy is not etched in stone; it's a fluid, dynamic tool that evolves with your nonprofit's needs, audience preferences, and platform changes. Regularly monitor your performance, using the metrics to make data-driven adjustments to your strategy. This agile approach allows your organization not only to reach its goals but also to harness the full power of social media's ability to connect and create change.

In conclusion, strategic planning remains a pivotal first step for nonprofits wishing to maximize their impact on social media. It brings clarity and direction to your efforts, ensuring each post, each platform, each interaction is a stepping stone towards your ultimate objectives. With carefully crafted SMART goals, a thorough understanding of your baseline position, a detailed tactical plan, a well-structured content calendar, and a commitment to continual monitoring and adjusting, your nonprofit can effectively wield the power of social media to amplify its impact and effect meaningful change.

Chapter 5. Know Your Audience: Analyzing and Engaging Your Followers

To optimally utilize social media for the benefit of your nonprofit, an understanding of your audience forms an essential foundation. This chapter illuminates how to identify, analyze, and engage your followers, an often overlooked but crucial aspect of strategic social media management, hence empowering your organization to send more resonating messages which ultimately have more impact.

5.1. The Importance of Knowing Your Audience

Understanding the characteristics of your audience equips you with valuable insights to craft compelling content that resonates with their interests, values, and viewpoints. When you are aware who constitutes your audience, you can readily tailor your online communications to meet their unique expectations, preferences, and needs. This way, you ensure your message is fine-tuned, targeting the right people at the right time with the right message.

Knowing your audience allows for improving donor participation, amassing volunteers, increasing event attendance, and fostering stronger relationships with your community. Further, it opens up an opportunity to expand your audience, as your content will be shared within networks of people who are likely to be interested in your cause.

5.2. Identifying Your Audience

Getting to know your audience starts with identifying who they are. Are they donors, volunteers, community members, other nonprofits, partners or beneficiaries of your work? In all likelihood, your audience is a mixture of all these segments. It's important to recognize that these segments might use social media platforms differently and have different content preferences.

Begin by identifying which social media platforms are most popular among your audience segments. Use analytics provided by the social media platforms themselves for this purpose. Facebook Insights, Twitter Analytics, Instagram Insights, and LinkedIn Analytics provide demographic information, including age, location, language, and more. This valuable, immediate feedback can be used to modify future social media strategies.

5.3. Analyzing Your Audience

After identifying your audience, the next step is to analyze them. Audience analysis involves studying the behaviors, preferences, habits, likes and dislikes of your audience. Social media platforms offer incredibly powerful analytical tools that provide detailed insights into your audience. These statistics can show you which posts gain the most engagement, when your audience is most active, what type of content they interact with most, and more.

Start with tracking your audience's activity patterns. Are they more active during the weekdays or the weekends? Is there a particular time of the day when they engage more with your posts? Studying these patterns can help you schedule your posts effectively.

Next, analyze the kind of posts that receive the maximum interaction. By identifying the features of these posts, you can replicate their success. These insights will shape the creation and delivery of future content, bringing it closer in line with what your audience loves.

5.4. Engaging Your Audience

Knowing your audience and understanding their preferences guide you in creating content that will captivates them. But beyond creating compelling content, you must also actively engage with your followers.

Engagement includes activities such as responding to comments, answering queries, sharing user-generated content, and acknowledging positive feedback. It's all about fostering a two-way communication that builds a sense of community among your followers.

When you consistently engage with your followers, it strengthens their affiliation with your cause and encourages further participation. Regular followers may turn into volunteers; volunteers may evolve into donors; donors may become ambassadors for your cause, spreading the word within their own networks.

You can also initiate specific engagement activities such as conducting online polls, Q&A sessions, hosting live videos, and more. Remember, there's no one-size-fits-all engagement strategy - it should be shaped by your audience analysis.

5.5. In Summary

In conclusion, the importance of knowing your audience in a nonprofit's social media strategy cannot be overstated. By identifying, analyzing, and engaging your audience, you can dramatically amplify your social media presence. Understanding who they are, what interests them, when they are most active and what they like or dislike lays the groundwork for a strong, effective social media strategy. Through active engagement, not only are you able to proliferate your cause effectively, but you also create a robust, vibrant online community that supports your mission. Acknowledge, interpret, and react to your followers, and be rewarded with a lively and engaged social media presence that amplifies the impact of your organization's work.

Chapter 6. Mastering Platforms: Characteristics, Strengths, and Weaknesses

The world of social media is as varied as it is vast. Each platform has its unique characteristics, strengths, and weaknesses, which can greatly influence the effect of your organization's efforts in engaging, informing, appealing, fundraising, or rallying your audience. Therefore, accurately understanding your platforms of choice will allow you to unlock their potential and use them to your benefit.

6.1. Understanding the Landscape

The contemporary digital landscape is populated with numerous social media platforms, each offering a unique avenue for communication and interaction. These platforms include the likes of Facebook, Twitter, Instagram, LinkedIn, YouTube, and Pinterest. Here, we will offer a comprehensive evaluation of these popular platforms and the unique strengths and weaknesses they present for nonprofit organizations.

6.2. Facebook

Facebook, the blue giant of the digital world, is a robust community-driven platform that offers unparalleled reach. With billions of users worldwide, it enables nonprofits to connect with a diverse audience and foster a sense of community among followers.

Strengths: The platform's strengths include its expansive user base, versatile post formats (text, photo, video, polls, live streaming), advanced targeting capabilities, and features such as Facebook Groups and Fundraising tools that specifically cater to nonprofits.

Weaknesses: On the downside, Facebook's algorithmic changes often affect content visibility, requiring an ongoing effort to stay updated. Also, the youth demographic is increasingly migrating to other platforms.

6.3. Twitter

Twitter is a platform known for its real-time updates and concise content format. It's an excellent space for raising awareness, engaging in public dialogues, and timely communications.

Strengths: Its strengths lie in its real-time nature, hashtag functionality for trend participation, and excellent opportunities for networking and public engagement.

Weaknesses: The 280 character limit can constrain message complexity, and the fast-paced nature can cause content to get lost in the feed. It also requires frequent postings to stay relevant.

6.4. Instagram

Instagram is a visually driven platform, popular with younger demographics. It's ideal for sharing stories through photos and short videos.

Strengths: Instagram encourages creative visuals and personal storytelling. It also enables hashtag use, has IGTV for longer videos and Instagram Live for real-time engagement.

Weaknesses: Instagram does not allow clickable links in the captions, directing traffic elsewhere might be a challenge. In-depth text-based information sharing is also limited.

6.5. LinkedIn

LinkedIn is a platform for professional networking and is an effective tool for organizations looking to engage with professionals and businesses.

Strengths: Its strengths lie in the professional networks, ability to publish in-depth articles, and features like LinkedIn Groups.

Weaknesses: However, it might not be the best platform for reaching a broader general audience or for casual, light-hearted content.

6.6. YouTube

YouTube is the prime platform for video content. It is great for sharing insightful documentaries, interviews, and instructional content.

Strengths: YouTube's strength is its video format which appeals to all demographics, its community features, and its powerful search engine capabilities due to Google's ownership.

Weaknesses: However, the creation of quality video content can be costly and time-consuming, and the platform is saturated with content competing for attention.

6.7. Pinterest

Pinterest is a unique platform centering on sharing and discovering new ideas. It is best for sharing visual content that directs traffic back to your website.

Strengths: Pinterest's strengths are in its visual discovery engine, the longevity of Pins, and its largely female user base for organizations targeting this demographic.

Weaknesses: However, it requires high-quality visuals and might not be suitable for conversation or community building.

6.8. Choosing Your Platforms

Your choices in social media platforms should reflect the nature of your nonprofit, the audience you wish to engage, and the type of content you intend to share. Evaluate your resources, manpower, and organizational goals, and choose platforms where you can regularly create and share high-quality content. Also, it's essential not to spread yourself thin by trying to be on all platforms but rather focus on a select few where you can truly shine and connect effectively with your audience.

Social media is an ever-evolving domain, and the rate at which new platforms emerge and existing ones evolve can be dizzying. However, a deep understanding of these platforms, their strengths and weaknesses, and staying adaptable allows you to steer your nonprofit's social media strategy toward success. With that, you are now ready to dive further into the social media universe and make an impactful splash in support of your noble cause!

Chapter 7. Crafting Compelling Content: Stories, Posts, and More

The creation of compelling content is the heartbeat of any successful nonprofit's social media strategy. The right posts can spark interest, stir emotions, inspire action, and foster a deep sense of connection with your audience. This chapter aims to provide a comprehensive roadmap for crafting material that resonates with your audience and amasses your desired impact.

7.1. Understanding the Importance of Compelling Content

Quality content is the cornerstone upon which successful social media campaigns are built. It enables nonprofits to precisely communicate their mission, spreading key messages and inspiring your digital community to take action. Compelling content has the power to enhance the visibility of your organization, amplify your voice, drive engagement, cultivate relationships with stakeholders, facilitate fundraising efforts and elevate your brand's reputation.

7.2. Know Your Audience

Before crafting your content, it's essential to understand your audience thoroughly. This understanding will guide you in developing stories and posts that speak to them. Segment your digital community based on parameters such as demographics, interests, or behaviors. Learn about their needs, preferences, and what kind of content appeals to them the most. Use social media analytics to gather these insights. A detailed audience persona will also aid you in personalizing content to build deeper connections.

7.3. Crafting a Content Strategy

Now that you've understood your audience let's anchor that knowledge into a concrete content strategy. Determine what kind of content aligns best with your nonprofit's mission and is likely to strike a chord with your audience. Is it emotion-evoking stories? Educational infographics? Interactive polls? Tailored posts for important days? The strategy should ideally strike a balance between what your organization wishes to convey and what the audience wishes to consume.

7.4. Telling Stories that Resonate

Storytelling can be an incredibly powerful tool for nonprofits. It humanizes your organization, generates empathy, and incites action far more than statistics or impersonal facts. Share the journey of your nonprofit, the success stories, the struggles, the grit, the change. These insights build trust with your followers, making them more likely to donate or volunteer.

7.5. Engaging with Videos and Images

Visual content, particularly video, can leave a lasting impact. Videos allow you to present dynamic and digestible snapshots of your work, whereas images can capture poignant moments flawlessly. While developing visual content, focus on quality over quantity. Use captions to add context to the visuals and remember to embed alt text for accessibility.

7.6. Leveraging User Generated Content

User-generated content (UGC) is content created by your followers that relates to your organization, such as photographs, testimonials, or social media posts. UGC adds authenticity to your narrative and fosters community engagement. Always credit the content creator and secure their permission prior to sharing.

7.7. Consistency is Key

Consistently posting on social media helps maintain visibility in your followers' feeds and keeps your mission fresh in their minds. A content calendar aids in planning your posts in advance and ensures you consistently share high-quality content.

7.8. Refining Your Voice and Tone

Your organization's voice and tone significantly influence how your followers perceive your brand. Your voice is your organization's personality, while your tone varies depending on the context of the post. Strive for a voice and tone that resonate with your demographic and reflect your mission authentically.

7.9. Call-to-Actions

Every piece of content you share should have a clear, compelling call-to-action (CTA). A persuasive CTA directs your followers exactly where you want them to go or what you want them to do, encouraging conversions.

7.10. Experimentation and Adaptation

Don't be afraid to experiment with different forms of content to see what resonates best with your audience. Social media trends evolve rapidly; staying flexible allows you to adapt and derive maximum benefits.

In conclusion, crafting compelling social media content is a mindful process that situates audience understanding at its core. With a focused strategy and a keen sense of experimentation, nonprofits can create content that truly resonates and compels their digital community towards action, amplifying their overall impact.

Chapter 8. Fundraising and Volunteer Recruitment on Social Media

As we begin to explore the realm of fundraising and volunteer recruitment on social media, it is essential to understand that the strategies employed within this chapter are not a one-size-fits-all model. They are tools and techniques that have been proven successful in various contexts and can be tailored to meet the unique needs and objectives of your nonprofit organization. Therefore, the emphasis throughout this chapter will be on providing a broad spectrum of options, interspersed with practical examples and actionable advice, all with an aim to empower your organization to carve its path in the digital space.

8.1. Understanding the Power of Social Media for Fundraising and Volunteer Recruitment

The initial part of this mission is to appreciate the overwhelming potential that social media platforms wield in fundraising and volunteer recruitment. With over half of the world's population using some form of social media, these platforms offer an unprecedented opportunity to reach a global audience. Moreover, they allow for quick dissemination of information, real-time engagement with supporters, and most importantly, they provide an accessible avenue for supporters to contribute to your cause, either through donations or by volunteering their time and skills.

However, using social media for effective fundraising and volunteer recruitment is not merely about posting a plea for help and expecting the donations and offers of assistance to flow in. It requires careful planning, strategic content creation, and thoughtful engagement with your audience.

8.2. Creating a Social Media Fundraising Strategy

Your organization's fundraising strategy on social media should be a well-thought-out plan that aligns with your overall organizational goals while leveraging the unique strengths of the platform being used. Consider the different fundraising options available on each platform, such as Facebook's 'Donate' button functionality, GoFundMe campaigns, or Instagram's donation stickers.

When creating a fundraising strategy, devote significant time and resources to content creation. Quality content that tells your organization's story, detailing why you need funds and explicitly stating how they will be used, is much more likely to resonate with potential donors.

Be explicit about your needs, but also demonstrate transparency. This can be done by communicating how donations have been utilized in the past and the impact they have had. This flowering of trust can convince your followers to transition from passive supporters into active donors.

8.3. Harnessing Social Media for Volunteer Recruitment

While financial contributions are crucial, the human resource is equally, if not more, valuable to a nonprofit organization. Social media platforms are fertile ground for unearthing individuals who genuinely care about your cause and are willing to go the extra mile to involve themselves actively.

When it comes to recruiting volunteers, employ a 'human-first' approach. This means rather than simply requesting volunteer assistance, you engage with potential volunteers, understand their interests and motivations, and highlight opportunities that would align with their skill set.

Visual storytelling is a very effective strategy in volunteer recruitment. Share images or videos of volunteers engaged in your organization's activities. Such firsthand accounts not only highlight the rewarding experience of volunteering with your organization, but also provide a firsthand glimpse of the impact they can make.

8.4. Social Media Tools and Best Practices for Fundraising and Volunteer Recruitment

Alongside the primarily human-centric approach, it is essential to leverage the tools and features offered by the different social media platforms for the most effective outcome. These include Facebook Fundraisers, Instagram Stories Donation Stickers, Twitter Chats for volunteer outreach, and LinkedIn's Volunteer marketplace, among others.

Furthermore, mastering best practices can result in a more focused and efficient approach to fundraising and volunteer recruitment. Some of these practices include leveraging social media analytics to understand your audience's behavior, hosting virtual events, acknowledging your donors and volunteers on your platforms, and capitalizing on relevant trends and viral moments.

While the potential of social media in these endeavors is immense, it is worth remembering that like all tools, these platforms will only yield results if used wisely, strategically, and respectfully. Constantly try to listen, learn, iterate, and improve to eventually reap the abundant benefits that social media promises for your nonprofit organization.

Chapter 9. Building Relationships: Networking and Collaboration Online

In this age of increasing interconnectivity and digital interactions, the architecture of online relationships is of paramount importance. It is this dynamic vitality, this intricate fabric, that shapes the success of a nonprofit organization's digital identity. In this complex realm of networking, collaboration, and online relations, the following guidelines and insight are presented.

9.1. The Art of Digital Networking

Digital networking, in its essence, is the act of establishing and maintaining relationships online for professional or organizational purposes. It's a pro-active approach where you reach out, make connections, and foster relationships with various stakeholders including potential donors, volunteers, other nonprofits, and influencers. This can be achieved through a myriad of ways such as engaging on their posts, sharing their content, attending virtual events and webinars, or connecting with them directly via messages.

The online realm gives you unlimited reach; anyone, anywhere in the world, can contribute to your cause if you effectively bridge the gap. Developing a diverse network of allies is often an excellent strategy for nonprofit growth. Different stakeholders can raise awareness about your cause in their respective communities, contribute resources, or collaborate on shared goals.

9.2. Strategies for Building Online Relationships

Maintaining online relationships is a critical part of networking. Presence and visibility matter, but engagement is the key. Engage with your followers through comments, likes, and shares, but don't shy away from starting conversations or creating discussions around important topics. Responding promptly and meaningfully to comments and messages can demonstrate that you value your audience and their input.

One strategy to cultivate online relationships is through influencer collaborations. After identifying potential influencers whose values align with your nonprofit's mission, propose a mutually beneficial partnership. This might involve them highlighting your cause in a series of posts or during events, in exchange for promoting them on your social media channels.

Remember that relationships are built on reciprocation and sincerity. Show genuine interest in your connection's work, and don't be afraid to ask them for advice or their perspectives on relevant topics.

9.3. Collaborations and Partnerships for Collective Impact

Virtual collaborations are not just about building relationships, but also leveraging those relationships to make an even more significant impact. Nonprofits function best by working collectively rather than competitively. Whether it's a coordinated social media campaign or an ongoing partnership, collaborations can help achieve common objectives.

Strategic partnerships with other nonprofits can expand your audience reach, generate new ideas, and even allow for cost sharing on larger projects or campaigns. Similarly, collaborations with corporates can have numerous benefits. Besides potential funding opportunities, corporate partnerships might offer pro-bono services, expertise, or even co-branded campaigns that can increase your visibility and reputation.

Ensure any partnership aligns with your mission and values to maintain the trust and support of your community. Be transparent about what each party brings to and gains from the partnership, and clearly communicate roles and expectations to avoid any potential conflict.

9.4. Leveraging Social Media Tools for Networking

Many social media platforms provide organizations with tools to facilitate networking. For instance, LinkedIn can be used to find potential collaborators or supporters in the professional realm, and the platform's Groups function can provide a niche community of like-minded individuals. Twitter Chats are a great way to meet and engage with those interested in particular topics, while Instagram's Live feature can be used to co-host discussions, interviews, or events.

Facebook groups are another channel for nonprofits to connect and collaborate with their target demographic in a more intimate and engaged virtual setting. They can offer an additional level of interaction, providing space for more detailed discussions, queries, and broader community engagement, further fostering an atmosphere conducive to relationship building.

9.5. In Conclusion: Continuity and Consistency

In a digitally connected world, the power of networking and collaboration cannot be overstated. Remember, digital relationships do not grow overnight. Like any relationship, it takes time, commitment, and consistent effort. However, the rewards – an active, engaged, and loyal online community, a network of influencers and collaborators, improved outreach, or effective campaigns – justify the continuous investment of time and resources.

Embrace the opportunities offered by social media, learn from your experiences, and keep refining your networking strategy. The digital landscape might be vast and ever-changing, but with intention, consistency, and a sprinkling of creativity, your nonprofit can create a robust online network that catalyzes significant change.

And within this journey, the words of Helen Keller echo truthfully, "Alone we can do so little; together we can do so much." And that, at its very core, is the power and potential of networking and collaboration in the digital-traversing realm maximizing an organization's capability to amplify impact and create change.

Chapter 10. Monitoring, Evaluating, and Improving Your Social Presence

Excellence in any field, including the digital landscape, requires ongoing evaluation and continuous attempts at improvement. To ensure your nonprofit organization is maximising its impact through social media platforms, it is integral to have an effective monitoring strategy. This includes evaluating your approach to digital identity, considering each strategic goal, and reviewing audience engagement. Most crucially, it involves consistent refining of your approach based on these evaluations.

10.1. Learning from Analytics

In the realm of social media, data is king. Social media platforms have powerful built-in analytic tools that can transform the way nonprofits operate. Facebook Insights, Instagram Insights, YouTube Analytics, and Twitter Analytics provide voluminous data to assess your social media campaigns' performances. They can help you track the reach of your posts, responses from your followers, and trends in followers' demographics and behavior.

For example, Facebook Insights delivers data about your posts, fan demographics, and fan engagement over a specified period. Instagram Insights offers a view of your followers' activities, including the times they are active, the content they interact with the most, and how they interact with it - this can include likes, comments, saves, and shares.

Making sense of these analytics involves identifying key performance indicators (KPIs) specific to your nonprofit's goals and objectives. Your KPIs could include measure of your post reach, follower growth rate, engagement rate, click-through-rate, conversion rate, bounce rate, or even the number of donations and volunteer registrations you receive through your social media campaigns.

By regularly reviewing these KPIs, you can gradually identify patterns and make strategic decisions for future campaigns. It also allows you to compare campaign outcomes and refine your social media strategy, ensuring that your online presence is both effective and dynamic.

10.2. Crafting Agile Strategies

While learning from analytics is about understanding your audience and their behaviors, crafting agile strategies is about adapting your approach based on this understanding. This involves quick decision-making and an openness to change. You should be willing to tweak your content strategy based on what your analytics reveal about your audience's interests and behaviors.

For example, if your older posts receive more engagement than newer ones, it might be time to revisit and replicate the characteristics of successful posts in your future content strategy. If a certain time of day generates more activity, consider scheduling your posts during these periods. If a certain type of content—say, volunteer success stories—attracts more interest, devote more resources to generating similar content.

Crafting agile strategies is, in essence, about never settling: always testing, always learning, and always improving.

10.3. Investing in Social Media Management Tools

While the native analytic tools of major social media platforms provide a substantial amount of data, investing in social media management tools can further streamline and enhance your evaluation processes. These tools often offer more detailed, cross-platform analytics that can inform your strategic decisions.

Tools like Hootsuite, Buffer, or Sprout Social can provide an overview of your social media performance across multiple platforms. They can also help schedule posts, track conversations, and generate detailed reports. With these tools, you can compare the performance of your nonprofit on different platforms, determine which platforms are the most effective for your cause and where your social media efforts should be focused.

Additionally, these tools usually have better capabilities for tracking the success of your specific campaigns. They can highlight the performance of your KPIs over time, giving you a better idea of what works and what doesn't.

10.4. Inviting Feedback and Encouraging Engagement

Monitoring and evaluating your social presence isn't solely about studying analytics. It also involves actively engaging with your audience and soaking in their feedback. You should invest time in keeping an eye on comments, messages, and shared posts.

By directly asking your followers for their opinions and experiences, you humanize your online presence and demonstrate that you value their feedback. Polls and surveys on social media platforms can be integral to this process, serving to collect valuable input expeditiously.

10.5. Case Study Analysis

Regularly researching and analyzing successful campaigns run by other nonprofits can provide valuable insights. Recognizing what strategies work for these successful campaigns and why they were effective can help inform your strategies and improve your own campaigns.

In conclusion, monitoring, evaluating, and improving your social media presence is a cyclical and ongoing process. By leveraging data, crafting agile strategies, investing in tools, inviting feedback, and learning from others, you can continuously refine and maximize your organization's digital footprint. No matter where you are in your social media journey, always remember that there's room for learning, growth, and improvement.

Chapter 11. Case Studies: Success Stories and Lessons Learned from Top Nonprofits

In any endeavor, learning from those who have walked the path before us can provide invaluable insights. Those successes we admire took risks, faced setbacks, and kept moving forward. Their journeys serve not only as motivation, but a roadmap as well. Let's use a lens to scrutinize the achievements of accomplished nonprofits leveraging social media, dig deeper into their strategies, and extract applicable lessons.

11.1. Charity: water's Unsung Heroes Campaign

Charity: water transformed the way donors perceived their contributions with their Unsung Heroes campaign. The campaign used social media to thank all do-gooders who had done selfless deeds to provide clean water, including volunteers, fundraisers, and the impoverished communities themselves.

They shared numerous visually captivating photos with emotional narratives encapsulating the struggles and triumphs encountered in their mission. This personalized approach allowed donors and followers to see exactly how their contributions were making real differences in people's lives. It also reinforced the message of community, the idea that every individual can contribute something powerful towards a cause.

Key takeaways:

- Adopt a storytelling approach. Weave a narrative that touches the heart, and present it visually and emotionally to engage your audience's empathy.

- Show the impact of contributions. The clearer donors see their impact, the more likely they'll be to continue supporting.

11.2. DoSomething.org's Straight Outta Compton Success

DoSomething.org has become famous among nonprofits for its successful youth campaigns that heavily utilize social media. In one of their most prominent endeavors, they sent out a call-to-action to American teens, asking them to donate their old school supplies to students in under-resourced areas. They named it after the movie "Straight Outta Compton."

The campaign was primarily promoted on Twitter and Instagram. The use of a catchy, current pop culture reference helped it gain traction quickly among the young internet-savvy demographics.

Key takeaways:

- Align your campaigns with current trends. This approach can increase resonance with modern audiences, especially the youth.

- Engage your audience with a straightforward call-to-action. Having a clear, specific, and actionable task encourages participation.

11.3. World Wildlife Fund's (#LastSelfie)

World Wildlife Fund (WWF) created a viral Snapchat campaign named #LastSelfie, aimed at drawing attention to endangered species. They shared 'selfies' of different animals accompanied with captions like "Better take a screenshot, this could be my #lastselfie."

The urgency and thought-provoking nature of the campaign prompted viewers to share and spread the message widely, leading to an increase in donations and global awareness about the plight of these species.

Key takeaways:

- Leverage the unique features of the platform you're using. For example, Snapchat's fleeting nature was used to emphasize the urgency of their cause.

- Elicit emotion in your followers. This increases the chances of your message being shared.

11.4. St. Jude Children's Research Hospital's Thanks and Giving

St. Jude utilized social media platforms impeccably to rally support for their annual fundraising campaign "Thanks and Giving." They shared stories of children who were battling or had overcome cancer. These vivid narratives, coupled with a compelling CTA to donate, resulted in extraordinary engagement from followers, stimulating a great surge in donations.

Key takeaways:

- Harness the power of storytelling. Real, personal, and vivid narratives establish a connection between your nonprofit and your audience.

- Include visible and compelling calls-to-action. They guide potential donors in the right direction, making the process of contributing as easy as possible.

11.5. Invisible Children's Kony 2012

Despite facing some criticism, Kony 2012 is one of the most successful nonprofit social media campaigns ever launched. The organizers capitalized on the power of video storytelling, creating a 30-minute long documentary exposing the crimes committed by Ugandan warlord Joseph Kony.

The campaign went viral worldwide, with over 100 million views in less than a week, and resulted in a significant increase in donations and advocacy actions striving to combat child soldier enslavement.

Key takeaways:

- The power of video storytelling is immense. Visual medium engages viewers and makes them more likely to share your content.

- Don't shy away from controversy. Exceptionally bold and daring campaigns often have the potential to go viral.

In conclusion, each campaign is unique, with its challenges and solutions. Yet, they all share a common trait: the strategic use of digital tools and platforms to communicate compelling narratives, transform passive viewers into devoted volunteers, and increase fundraising. As your nonprofit embarks on its own social media journey, keep these success stories in mind – they are proof that, with creativity and perseverance, you can use digital platforms to amplify your mission and impact. The potential for social media to drive change and progress is immense - it's time for you to harness it.

www.ingramcontent.com/pod-product-compliance
Lightning Source LLC
Chambersburg PA
CBHW062309290526
45794CB00006B/2739